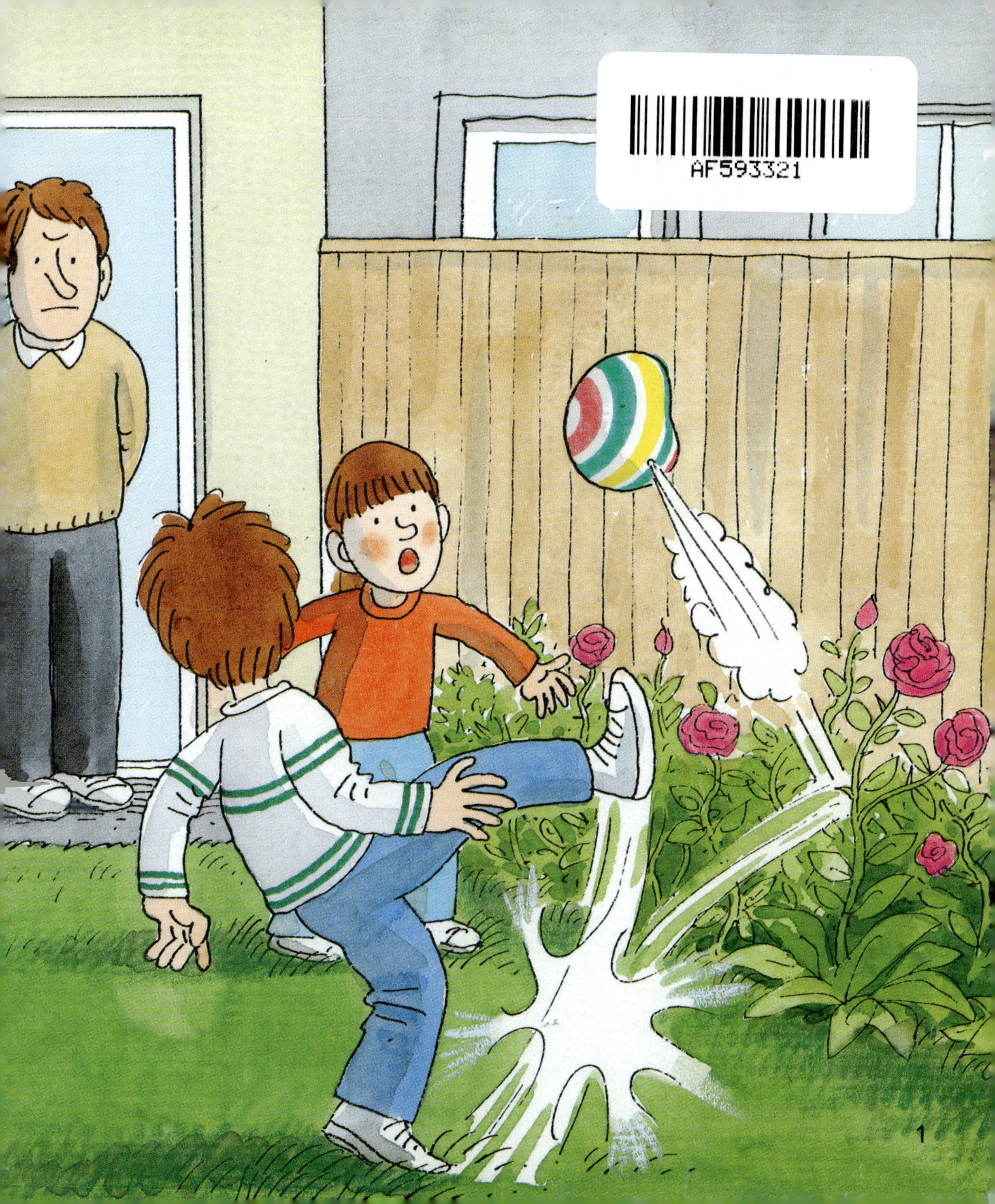

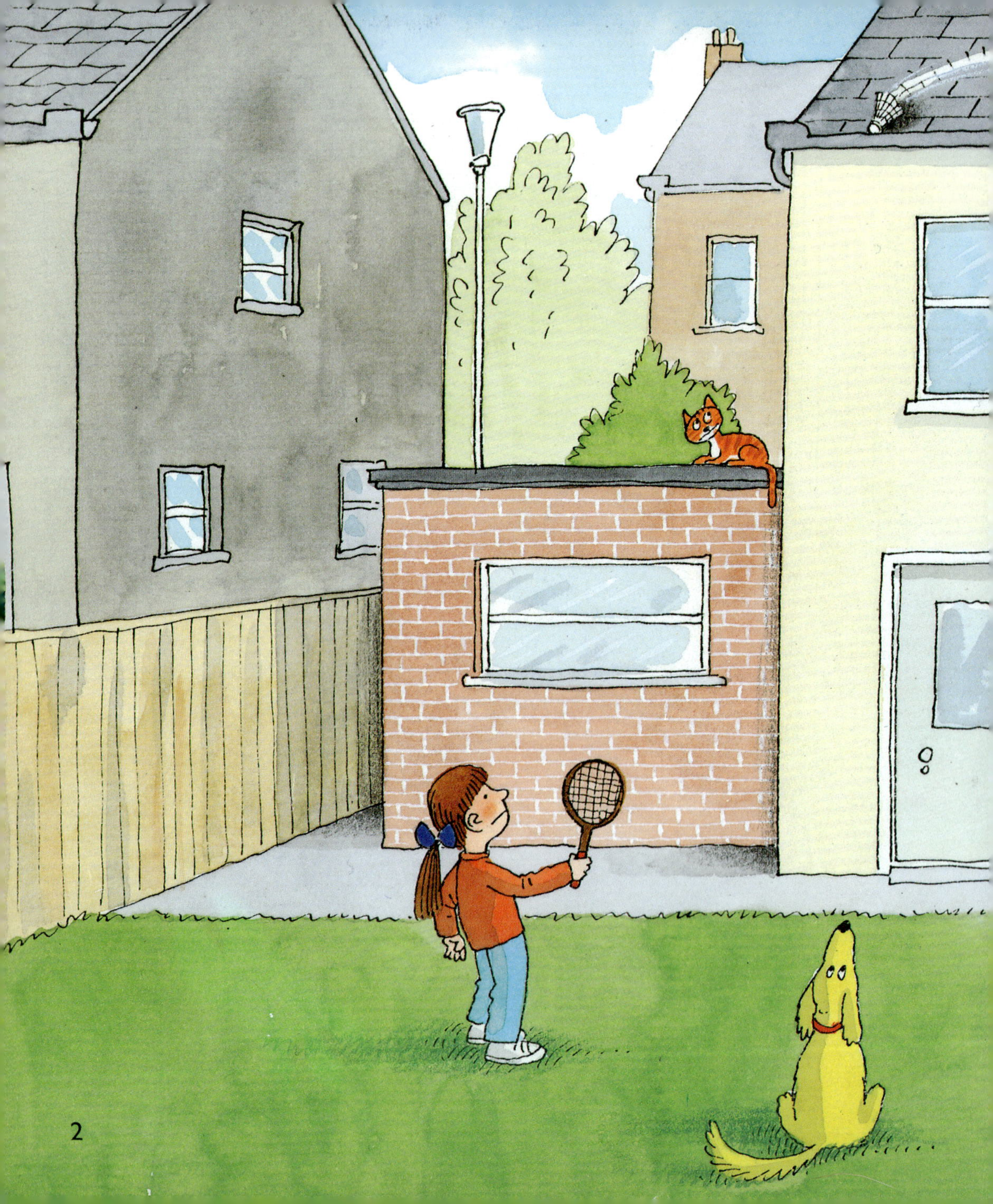

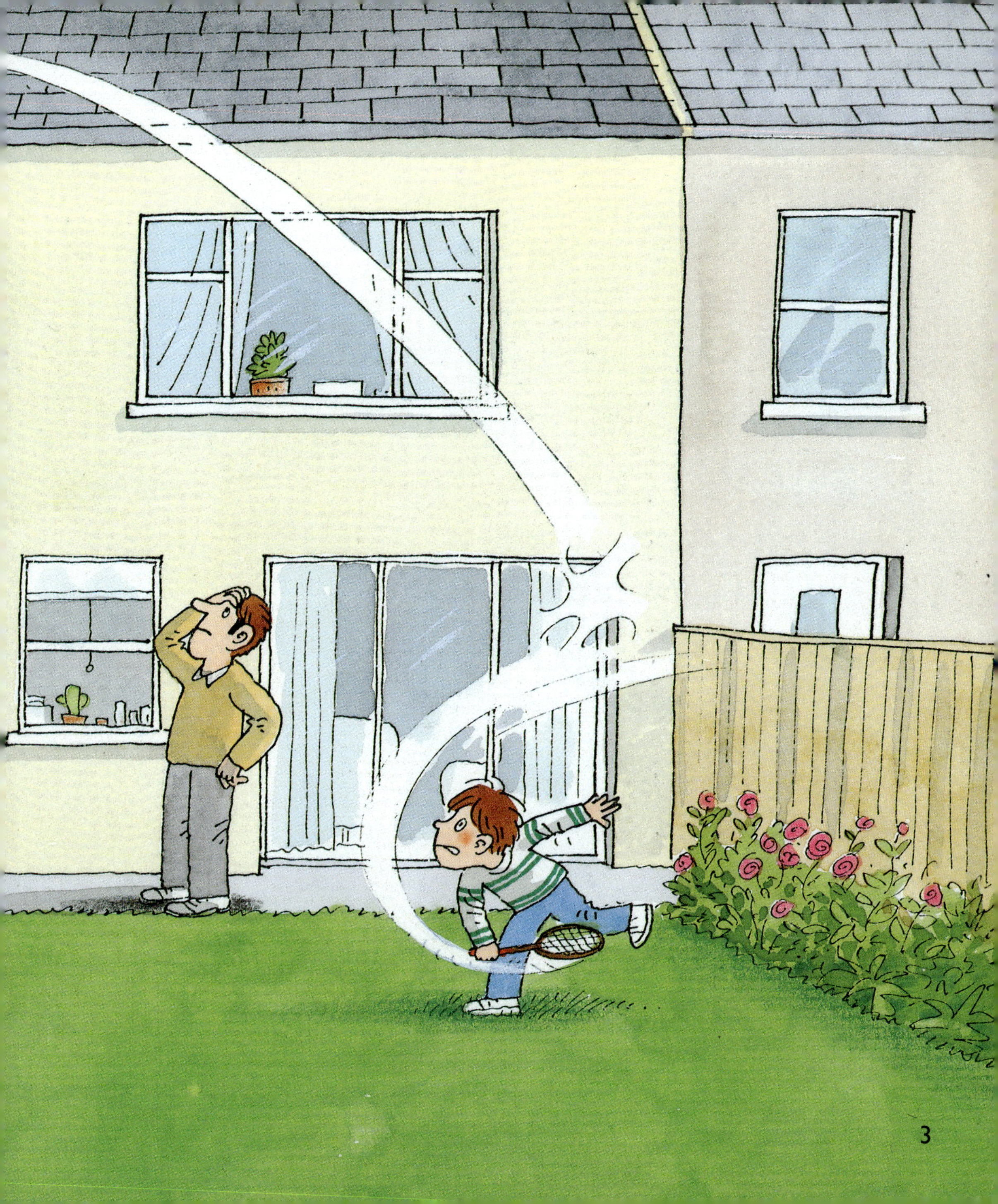

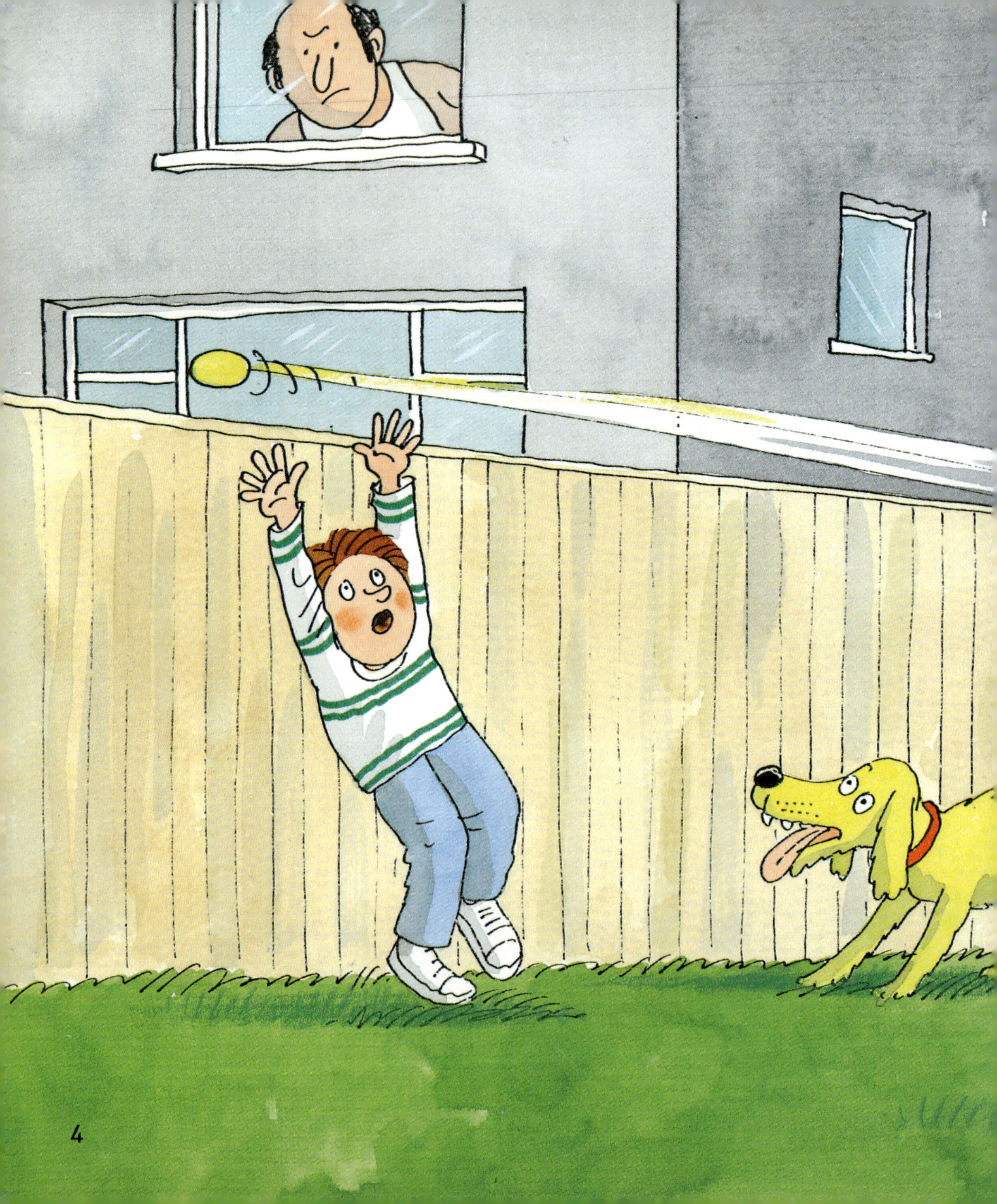

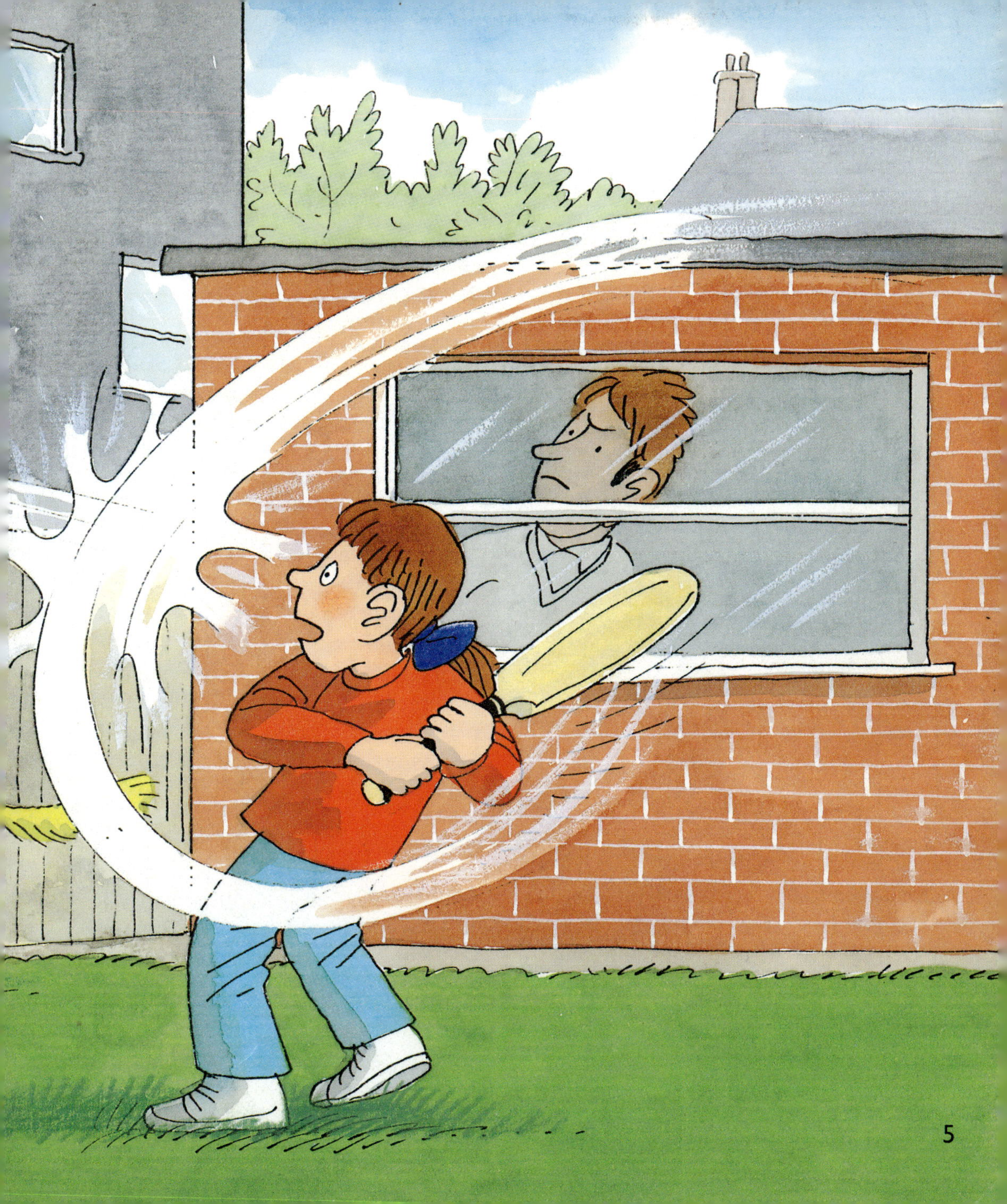

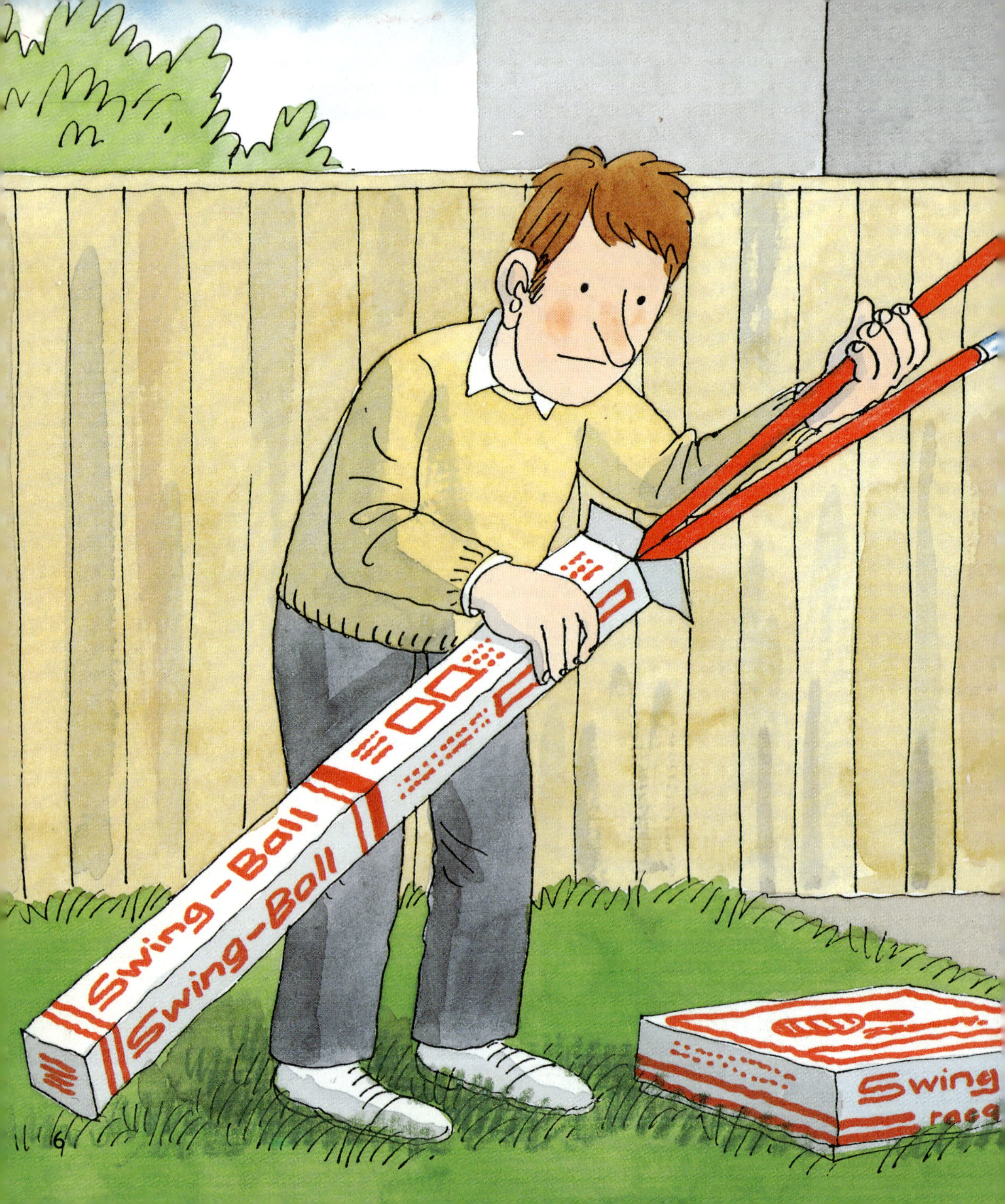
Swing-Ball
Swing-Ball
Swing

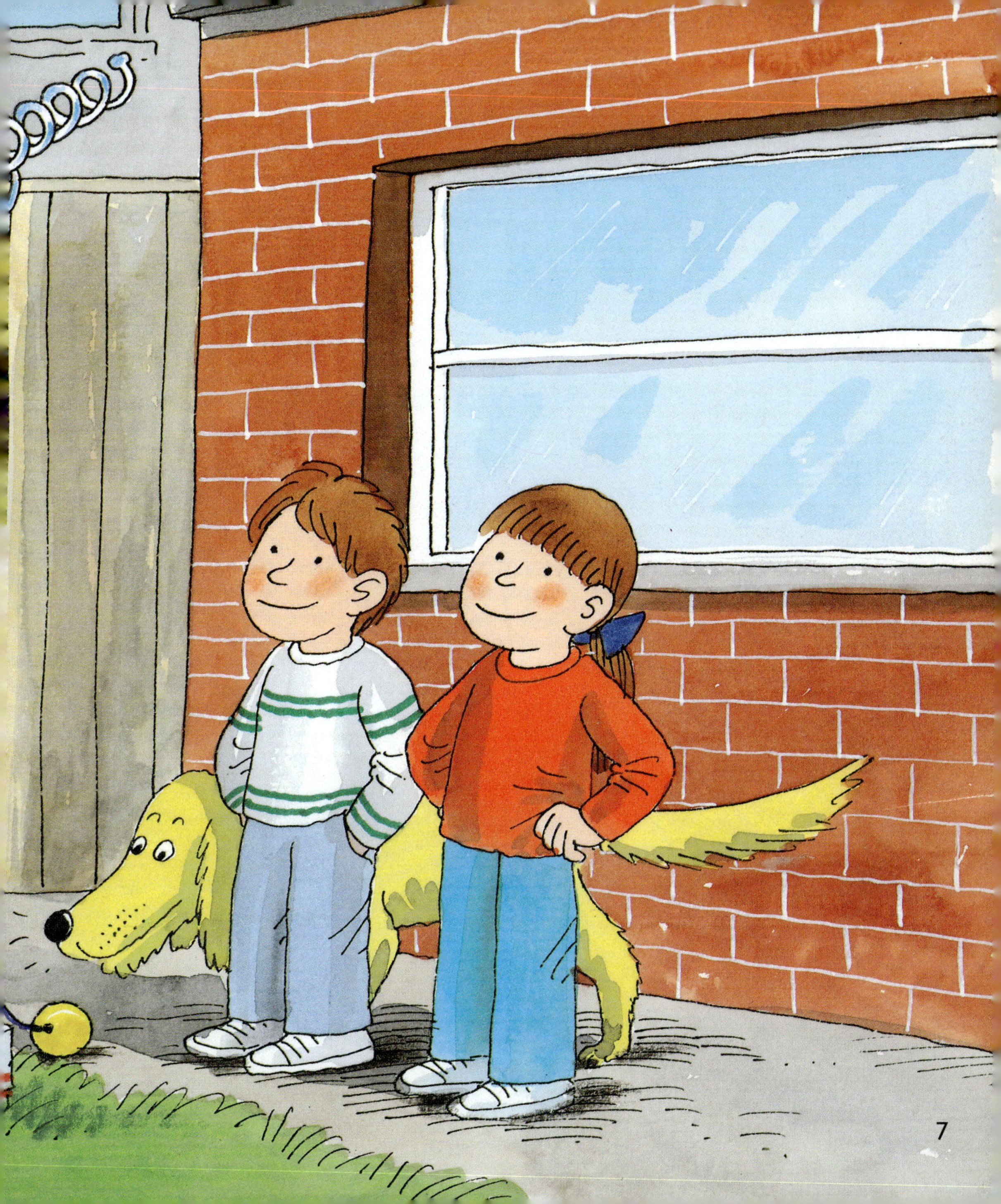

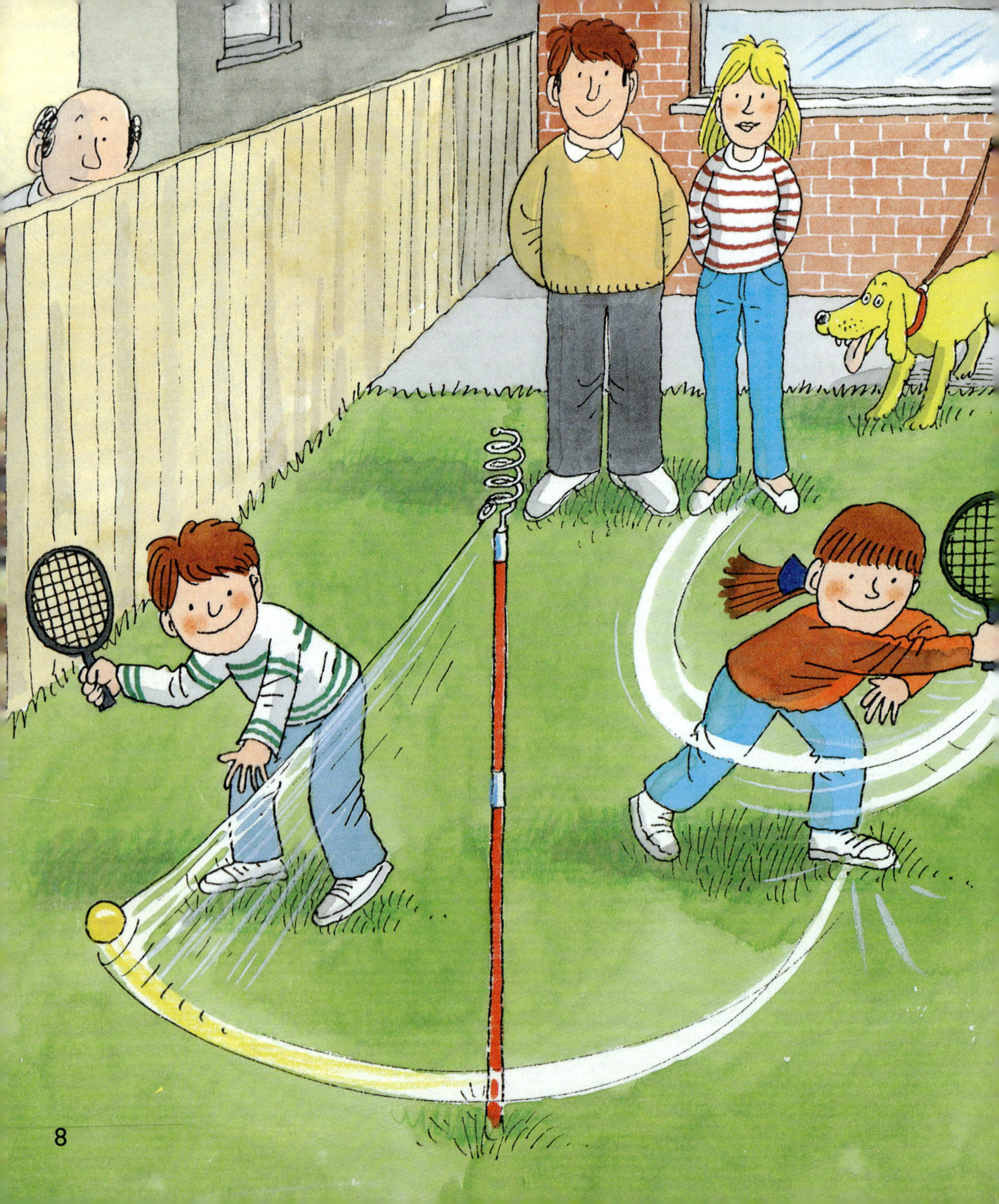